Thin as Air

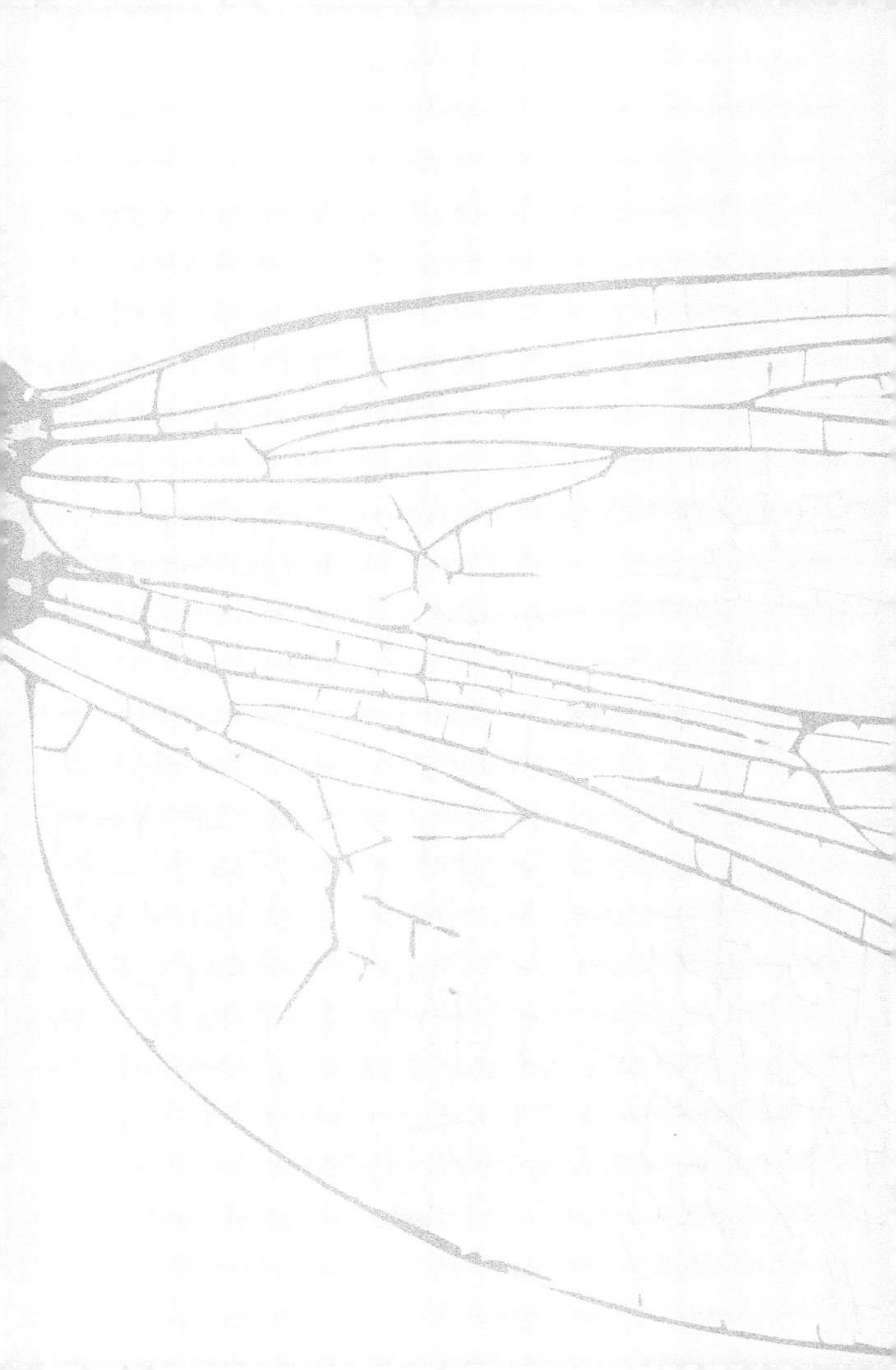

Thin as Air

poems

ELLIE ALTMAN

Salt Water Media
29 Broad Street
Berlin, Maryland 21811

Copyright © 2025 Ellie Altman

All rights reserved. No part of this publication may be reproduced, distributed, or transmitted in any form by any means, including photocopying, recording, or other electronic methods without the prior written permission of the author, except in the case of brief quotations embodied in reviews and certain other noncommercial uses permitted by copyright law. For permission requests, write to the author at the email address below.

ellie@elliealtmanpoet.com

ISBN 979-8-218-65081-0

Published by Salt Water Media
Edited & designed by Lindsay Lusby
Typeset in Cormorant Garamond & Adobe Caslon Pro
Cover photo used with permission from iStock
Title page photo used with permission from Adobe Stock
Author photo by Kris Kelley

Printed in the United States of America

First Printing, 2025

CONTENTS

Her Morning Poem (She Wears Pearls to Breakfast)	1
Recipe for a New Hairdo	3
My Avatar, the Water Bug	5
First Dance	7
Riding in the Back Seat	9
Unfurling a Metamorphosis	11
Like It or Not	12
Been There, Done That	14
Her Scales	15
Skin and Bone	17
When I Hired a Labor Lawyer	18
Inventory	20
Upon Entering Her Eighth Decade	22
Nourishment	24
How I Became a Stewing Chicken	26
Caught Growing Old	28
We Are Generation Perennials	30
Like Mother, Like Daughter	31
Acknowledgments	33

Her Morning Poem
(She Wears Pearls to Breakfast)

> *Hello, sun in my face,*
> *Hello, you who made the morning . . .*
> *Watch, now, how I start the day*
> *in happiness, in kindness.*
> —Mary Oliver, "Why I Wake Early"

It was years in the making, her morning routine.
A gentle alarm: the sound of spring peepers.
Four a.m., still too early to rise. Thirty minutes later,
a soft vibration from her watchband nudges. The rising hour
is near. The nudge repeats at five a.m., only a few minutes left
to stroke her dog, curled in a sleeping knot snug against her back.
Then she remembers to smile, thwarting the tiniest angst
about the day to come. Rough sketches of poems
raise and wave their hands seeking her attention
like eager students seated in the classroom's front row.

Lying in bed on her back, she first stretches her legs
in phantom bicycle pedals and next makes the large strides
of a cross-country skier, then hugs her knees tightly

against her chest. Pleased with the prospects
of the day and limber enough to take the morning's first steps.
She gathers her bedside reading, phone, and juice cup.
Slips her bare feet into well-worn Birkenstocks.

At the small bathroom counter, a tight galley between
the tub and sink, she stretches her arms overhead,
welcoming the day as if feeling sun on her face.
She pliés down and back up: twenty grand pliés.
Wrapping her arms around her shoulders to touch her wings
then reaching above her head to wings-flung-open.
Repeating back and forth, practicing the rhythm
of comfort and aspiration the day is apt to bring.
More thoughts about her morning poem, she smiles again.

A splash of tepid water removes decades from
the seasoned landscape of her face
with a palm of warm golden jojoba oil and a prayer:
> *I forgive the signs of my trespasses.*
She dries her skin gently, blesses herself.
Rubbing her nails, hands, feet, and smoothing her face,
she glistens with more thoughts of her morning poem.

She hangs her nightgown on its appointed hook
behind the bathroom door, pulls on dancer's tights.
The dark second skin stretched taut defies gravity's
tragic ballet, aging skin's dimples and sags.
She turns back to the dresser for small black pearl earrings.
Now readied, she descends the stairs
to begin her morning poem.

Recipe for a New Hairdo

Ingredients:
1. unwashed, unkempt hair
2. sea salt-infused hairspray
3. a collection of hair picks
4. a collection of hair clips

Directions:
1. spritz sea salt hairspray, daily
2. rest head on feather pillow overnight, forming kinks, curls, and frizz
3. fluff hair using hair picks, accentuating kinks, curls, and frizz
4. clip hair loosely off face with hairpins (as many as needed) behind the crown of the head
5. repeat daily: spritz, rest, fluff, and clip

To try on a new persona,
she sculpts her hair
into a bed hairdo—
coveting thick curls,
the opposite of her
cotton-candy frizzy-do.

Voilà!
Like a tiara,

her own trophy hair.
Like a bad-ass girl
wrapping her soft, wide rump
in tight jeans with frayed patches
and embroidery.
Her crown coifed naturally
by whatever she never does—
neither shampoo nor brush.
Her new persona shouts:
Shake your booty!

My Avatar, the Water Bug

Spinning, skidding afloat
across the calm pond's surface tension,

balancing on water droplets.
Racing, darting lightness—

weightless acrobats,
on a high wire,

magicians of distraction
shuffling cards for a new reality,

vibrating with the wet skin's buoyancy.
At play with physics,

testing material reality's nonexistent edges—
a constant sharing and redefining,

ever-changing identity.
You ask:

Is the water bug the water?
Is the water the water bug?

And we ask: *Where do we begin?*
Where do we end?

First Dance

Me at five,
when my mother still has time
to mother full-time,
before the divorce.
She takes me to watch a dance class
down a ruddy, dirt drive
hidden beneath tall oaks
in a leafy neighborhood.

Dozens of soft, bare feet pattered
on the wide, wooden planks
of a large playroom.
Dressed in simple, sleeveless tunics—
silky pink, clipped at the waist
with a narrow elastic band.

Sitting on the next to last step—
chin resting on my knees,
right shoulder braced
against the railing—
I watch intently
between the spindles.
Would you like to dance? she asks.

I can't speak.
Nodding vigorously:
Yes, yes, yes.

Me, on that day,
mesmerized by the girls' rapid circling,
as if lifting the room from its foundation.
She, on that day,
opening a window
to show me a boundless world
beneath a cloudless sky.

Riding in the Back Seat

The photo sits on my desk in a silver frame,
as if she were mine.
She is traveling in the back seat of the family's Plymouth sedan—
passing suburbs of ranchers and split-levels
filled with families with safe stories.

A married mother and father at every dinner table,
world news delivered by Walter Cronkite,
eggs by the egg-man,
milk by the milkman,
mail by the mailman.

Her head rests by the open window,
her face brushed peaceful by the breeze.
She is a single ginger lily in full bloom
on a sun-soaked window ledge.

A Sunday drive, settling calm,
an afternoon of grace.
An unknown world held at bay
by her father at the wheel.

He asks: *A penny for your thoughts?*
She has no thoughts.
Letters she tries to knead into words
crumble between her fingers,
falling through cracks in the floor.

Below, the Earth moves.
Above, storm clouds gather.
And she, speechless, in the ominous in-between.

Unfurling a Metamorphosis

Middle class teaches you
to wait your turn,
postpone pleasure,
eat dessert after your vegetables,
save the best for last.

There is no dress rehearsal
for the act of stretched-taut fledging
that carries you
out of the nest
with few buffers from the world's brutality—

rebellion becoming rampage,
rage becoming scarlet wound,
sores becoming rotten flesh.
And you become gaunt and hungry,
wrapped in a translucent skin
with your underside exposed.

Yet the moment arrives when,
inevitably, you grow wings
and take flight to the next landing
and the next.

Like It or Not

Your body betrays and rewards.
Like your young mother—
      rapping your knuckles for a childish prank,
      then assuring you of your true worth,
      feeding you every morning
a soft-boiled egg and cinnamon toast.

Like your garden through the seasons—
      barren in winter,
      budding in spring,
      explosive in summer,
      and subdued in fall
under the cover of saffron and burgundy.

Like your first lover—
      offering bouquets on special occasions,
      withholding his affection unexpectedly,
      coming and going to his own refrain.

Like your wooden yoyo—
      winding up and down,
      wobbling on its string,
      then falling to a dangling halt.

Like a gamble with a dice-throw
and your unsteady first step.

Been There, Done That

Been in some seedy bathrooms
behind cinderblock bars and gas stations but

never witnessed a brawl nor seen
rivulets of blood and guts in the aftermath of a beating.

Just discovering the car keys mistakenly stashed
in the wrong pocket or an extra shoelace where routinely

the credit card is kept for the gas pump
leads to a personal disturbance of the proportions

of a gravitational vibration stirring something unremarkable
that becomes the mother of just the opposite

like fingerprints on heirloom wine glasses,
dressed in favorite linen trousers, wrinkled and worn at the knees.

I divert my eyes, willing myself to be proud
when I am actually undone.

Her Scales

Each morning,
she weighs in.

She walks briskly two blocks
to the corner grocery,

cautiously stepping onto the worn mat
at its automatic door entrance.

She looks ahead, chin up,
and imagines this time

her weight is not enough
to trigger the door's opening.

Left barred from entering
yet validated—

her goal weight
in meager and rich times,

before arrivals and after departures
for and from life's events,

through the small arcs of her days
with friends and strangers.

She weighs her worth
at automatic doors.

Skin and Bone

Curvy Titan goddesses are not my Polaris,
preferring to follow the ectomorphic aesthetic—

Lisbeth Salander, reclusive and feisty
with her dragon tattoo, and Joan Didion,

living on cola and cigarettes with her anorexic,
coke-habit look, her bad-girl photo in the LA sun

leaning against her Daytona-yellow Corvette Stingray.
Salander—an acrobat who kicks evil in the balls—

her appendages' delicacy is deceptive,
holding mythical power of revenge.

And Didion—of the sophisticated literocracy—
deftly darts on surfaces into a disappearing act,

gathering observations without leaving a trace—
defiant witches living on air.

When I Hired a Labor Lawyer

Like back-seat drivers, they warn me:
Prepare for your reputation raked raw,
your spirit shattered into shards,
and you cooked over crimson coals.

I know, I know—
I've made it this far,
kept the door ajar,
preparing to lose all.

I know, I know—
It's an old story:
White Mean vs. White Hair in Tennis Shoes.
Never ends well for the
dog held under.

I know, I know.
I estimate at this rate, on my court date,
I'll weigh one hundred and two.
Walking my dog for the hours I used to earn my living,
I've lost the weight of an arm.

They have deep pockets,
well-connected golf buddies,
and blustering bravado
that will drain your savings.
Don't expect pity.

I know, I know.
I'll walk through the door,
take my seat.
I'll rub my smoky quartz
and breathe deep to levitate
above the fray.
Visualize a guardian angel
erecting a bully-proof shield.

There must be a conspiracy.
It will undo you.

I know, I know.
When the robed man behind the desk rules,
I'll be almost transparent at one hundred and two.

Inventory

She cleans most mornings,
surveying her house's wood floors
for her life's inventory of scratches and scars.

When the iron fell from the ironing board,
leaving a huge gash
on the laundry room floor.

When three cans of coconut milk
slipped from her arms
making half-moon dents
on the pantry floor.

When she was drying it,
she lost her grip and the butcher knife fell,
making a big ding next to the floor mat
at the kitchen sink.

And when the dog barks uncontrollably
and races full tilt from the front door
to the porch door to the back door,
scoring a pattern of scratches that marks the path

for warding off attack from the mail carrier,
lest she dares to enter the house.

Her whole life carved out
on these floors, yet
no blood spilt,
no pain felt—
only the pull of gravity
and its everyday violence.

Upon Entering Her Eighth Decade

It is not the body parts
that have gone south—
the skin folding
over my knees,
breasts shrunken
over my ribs,
hair balding
at the temples—
not these inevitabilities.

It is the memories.
In midlife, I lost all the details.
But now, in my lateness, they crash like waves
and create floods that rise to my knees,
embarrassing myself in front of others
with revelations of these details,
as if deserving a megaphone
or headlines above the fold,
precise as a photograph
and its caption of who stands
left to right.

The reliving has become the present—
a life fulfilled after all.
I relish these moments
of no consequence—
a reliving of my ephemeral being on this Earth,
the last gasp
as I begin to prepare
to disappear into thin air.

Nourishment

The older she is, the skinnier she becomes,
with so many meals to miss.

Because the call about an emergency comes
just as the pasta water starts to boil.

Because she oversleeps
and the train leaves in twenty minutes.

Because their argument over the school board contest
ruins her appetite.

Because the effort doesn't seem worth it
when there are leftovers in the refrigerator.

Because disgust with the day's disappointments
sends her to bed before dark.

Because her stomach quivers with butterflies
over the public speaking engagement at seven.

Because she is swooning over a new love
and that's plenty of nourishment to fill her belly.

Because a storm is coming across the lake
and watching this drama arrive is mesmerizing and she forgets.

Because she stays in the garden
doing one more task,

leaving only enough time to take a bath
and curl up in bed to read the final chapter.

Her arms cross her thin torso,
fingers touching her wings.

She stares at the high ceiling above and asks:
Am I satiated?

How I Became a Stewing Chicken

        Its legs splayed,
the freshly roasted chicken is tender and done.
        Its crispy skin falls from the meat
into my washed hands.
        Its fat, the lushest cuticle cream,
a balm soothing my seventy-year-old skin,
        slippery and glistening,
tempting me to finger-lick over the kitchen sink.

        My thoughts move beyond its proud, bosomy body—
bred as a Dolly Parton impersonator—
        to my own boyish one, approaching fat-free.
Stringy with its small muscles, tendons, and bones exposed
        like a chicken's legs or wings.
With time and a mix of genes, dog-walking, feeding, and aging,
        my shins and calf muscles are revealed,
wrapped in tissue-thin skin—
        freckled, bruising easily.

I am an old bird, lithe and gristly,
        with scant fat
that makes a chicken delicious,
        yet still clucking and darting

about a crowded barnyard,
> gossiping with the other hens,
scratching for grubs and pecking at seeds,
> no time to waste,
and a body built for soup stock.

Caught Growing Old

When do we stop growing up and start
  growing old? Years of denial until
    a reflection reveals the evidence.

Not a birthday. Not a rite of passage.
  No marching band parading down Main Street.
    No jugglers. No flying monkeys.

No stampeding bulls. No footrace
  there and back. No animal sacrificed.
    No blood spilled. No feast.

No crystal shattered. No large bills
  slipped into your palm. No easing into.
    Applying ourselves without a curriculum—

yet, with a license granted for a new awakening.
  Stepping onto the stage of a wide-angle-lens
    panorama, all at once, the horizons in the surround

spin from gold to ruby to cobalt.
  Staring down the narrowing shaft
    of growing older, where hillsides

of waning summer blooms deepen to autumn's sunset.
It takes several breaths to extinguish the blaze
of six dozen birthday candles.

We Are Generation Perennials

We are still here
blossoming again and again—
a new model for living
where we take stage,
then take breaks.

Nourished by sun, moisture, and rich soil,
perennials live for decades,
even generations—
always aspirational.

Shifting away from fear of the late season,
nestling beneath fallen leaves
into winter's sleep,
sending our energy to our roots
to prepare to re-emerge,
to live well and long.

Like Mother, Like Daughter

During the mother's orange craze,
she paints the front door creamsicle.

Now the daughter muses about orange
from the driver's seat of her Volvo station wagon.

With leather seats to match a baseball mitt,
and her dog, Miss Sweet Potato Pie, in the far back,

she is dressed in an autumn sunset skirt and
a persimmon silk scarf draped around the neck.

With an amber pendant necklace and
an apricot clutch in her lap,

she checks the rearview mirror.

ACKNOWLEDGMENTS

Grateful acknowledgment is given to the editors of the following publications in which these poems first appeared, sometimes in slightly different forms.

Gyroscope Review: "How I Became a Stewing Chicken"
The Shore: "Inventory"

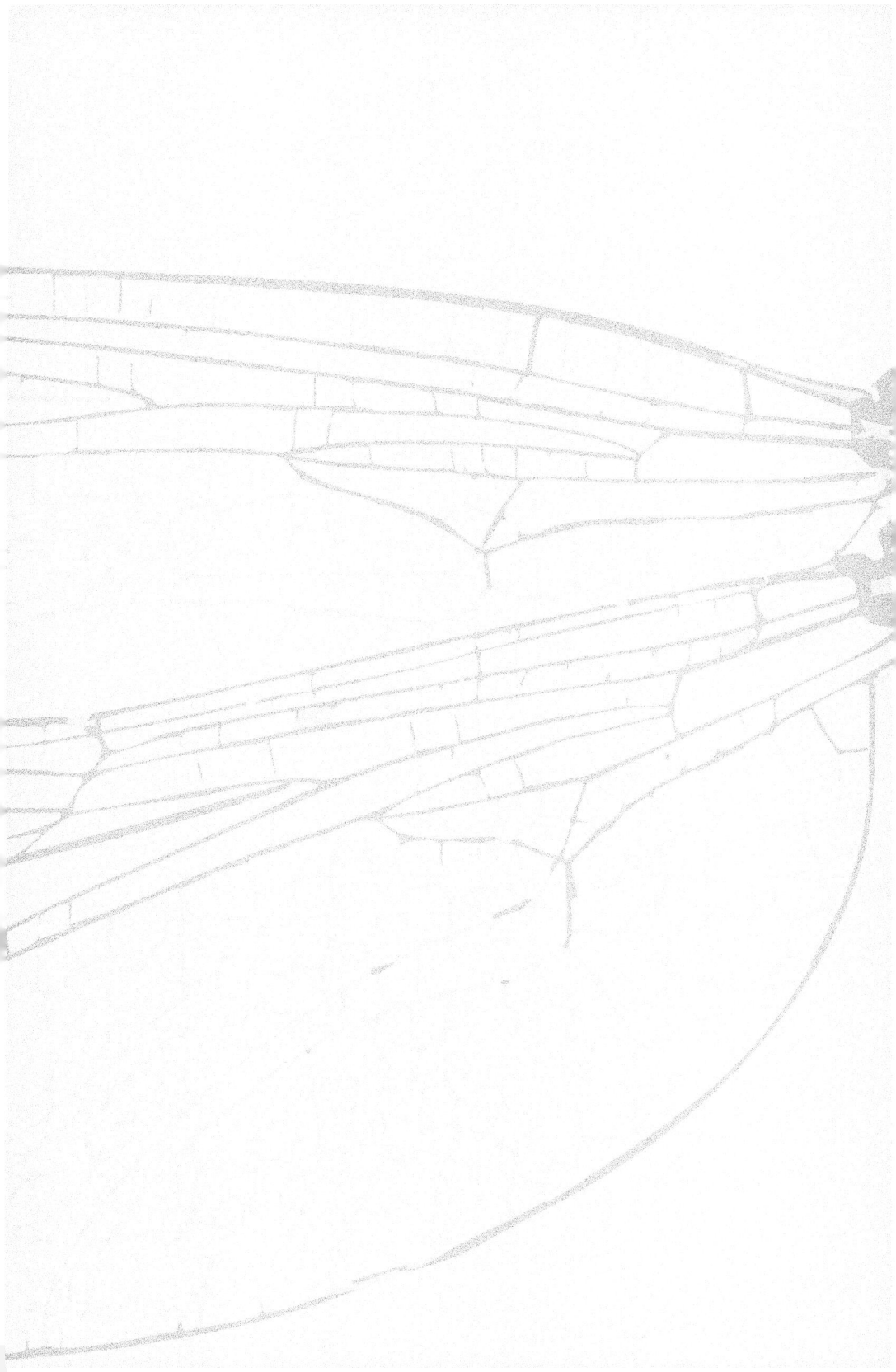

www.ingramcontent.com/pod-product-compliance
Lightning Source LLC
Chambersburg PA
CBHW050822090426
42737CB00022B/3478